Alaric Alfred Watts

Al. Watts on dogs; their habits, characteristics, and diseases

Alaric Alfred Watts

Al. Watts on dogs; their habits, characteristics, and diseases

ISBN/EAN: 9783337814779

Printed in Europe, USA, Canada, Australia, Japan

Cover: Foto ©ninafisch / pixelio.de

More available books at **www.hansebooks.com**

AL. WATTS

ON

DOGS ;

THEIR HABITS, CHARACTERISTICS, AND DISEASES.

BOSTON, MASS.:
AL. WATTS, 164 LINCOLN STREET.
1876.

INTRODUCTORY CHAPTER.

Origin. — General Characteristics. — Habitat. — Varieties. — F. Cuvier's
Divisional Arrangement. — Arrangement adopted by the Author.

FROM the earliest times we have reason to believe that the dog has
been the faithful companion and assistant of man in all parts of the
world, and his fidelity and attachment are so remarkable as to have
become proverbial. Before the introduction of agriculture, it was
by means of the hunting powers of this animal that man was enabled
to support himself by pursuing the wild denizens of the forest; for
though now, with the aid of gunpowder, he can in great measure dis-
pense with the services of his assistant, yet, until the invention of that
destructive agent, he was, in default of the dog, reduced to the bow and
arrow, the snare or the pitfall. The dog was also of incalculable service in guarding the flocks and herds from the depredations of the
Carnivora, and even man himself was often glad to have recourse to
his courage and strength in resisting the lion, the tiger, or the wolf.
Much has been written on the origin of the dog, and Pennant, Buffon,
and other naturalists have exhausted their powers of research and invention in attempting to discover the parent stock from which all are
descended. The subject, however, is wrapped in so much obscurity as
to baffle all their efforts, and it is still a disputed point whether the
shepherd's dog, as supposed by Buffon and Daniel, or the wolf, as con-
jectured by Bell, is the progenitor of the various breeds now existing.
Anyhow, it is a most unprofitable speculation, and, being unsupported
by proof of any kind, it can never be settled upon any reliable basis.
We shall not, therefore, waste any space in entering upon this discus-
sion, but leave our readers to investigate the inquiry, if they think fit,
in the pages of Buffon, Linnæus, Pennant, and Cuvier, and our most
recent investigator, Professor Bell. It may, however, be observed that
the old hypothesis of Pennant that the dog is only a domesticated jackal,
crossed with the wolf or fox, though resuscitated by Mr. Bell, is now
almost entirely exploded; for while it accounts somewhat ingeniously
for the varieties which are met with, yet it is contradicted by the stub-
born fact that, in the present day, the cross of the dog with either of
these animals, *if produced*, is incapable of continuing the species when
paired with one of the same crossed breed. Nevertheless, it may be
desirable to give Mr. Bell's reasons for thinking that the dog is descended from the wolf, which are as follows : — '

"In order to come to any rational conclusion on this head, it will be necessary to ascertain to what type the animal approaches most nearly, after having for many successive generations existed in a wild state, removed from the influence of domestication, and of association with mankind. Now we find that there are several instances of the existence in dogs of such a state of wildness as to have lost even that common character of domestication, variety of color and marking. Of these, two very remarkable ones are the dhole of India and the dingo of Australia. There is, besides, a half-reclaimed race amongst the Indians of North America, and another also partially tamed in South America, which deserve attention. And it is found that these races in different degrees, and in a greater degree as they are more wild, exhibit the lank and gaunt form, the lengthened limbs, the long and slender muzzle, and the great comparative strength which characterizes the wolf; and that the tail of the Australian dog, which may be considered as the most remote from a state of domestication, assumes the slightly bushy form of that animal.

"We have here a remarkable approximation to a well-known wild animal of the same genus, in races which, though doubtless descended from domesticated ancestors, have gradually assumed the wild condition; and it is worthy of special remark that the anatomy of the wolf, and its osteology in particular, does not differ from that of the dog in general, more than the different kinds of dogs do from each other. The cranium is absolutely similar, and so are all, or nearly all, the other essential parts; and, to strenghten still further the probability of their identity, the dog and wolf will readily breed together, and their progeny is fertile. The obliquity of the position of the eyes in the wolf is one of the characters in which it differs from the dog; and, although it is very desirable not to rest too much upon the effects of habit on structure, it is not perhaps straining the point to attribute the forward direction of the eyes in the dog to the constant habit, for many successive generations, of looking forward to his master, and obeying his voice."*

Such is the state of the argument in favor of the original descent from the wolf, but, as far as it is founded upon the breeding together of the wolf and dog, it applies also to the fox, which is now ascertained occasionally to be impregnated by the dog; but in neither case we believe does the progeny continue to be fertile if put to one of the same cross, and as this is now ascertained to be the only reliable test, the existence of the first cross stands for nothing. Indeed, experience shows us more and more clearly every year, that no reliance can be placed upon the test depending upon fertile intercommunion, which, especially in birds, is shown to be liable to various exceptions. Still it has been supported by respectable authorities, and for this reason we have given insertion to the above extract.

GENERAL CHARACTERISTICS.

In every variety the dog is more or less endowed with a keen sight, strong powers of smell, sagacity almost amounting to reason, and considerable speed, so that he is admirably adapted for all purposes connected with the pursuit of game. He is also furnished with strong teeth, and courage enough to use them in defence of his master, and with muscular power sufficient to enable him to draw moderate weights, as we see in Kamtschatka and Newfoundland.

HABITAT.

In almost every climate the dog is to be met with, from Kamtschatka to Cape Horn, the chief exception being some of the islands in the Pacific Ocean ; but it is only in the Temperate Zone that he is to be found in perfection, the courage of the bulldog and the speed of the greyhound soon degenerating in tropical countries. In China and the Society Islands dogs are eaten, being considered great delicacies, and by the ancients the flesh of a young fat dog was highly prized, Hippocrates even describing that of an adult as wholesome and nourishing. In a state of nature the dog is compelled to live on flesh, which he obtains by hunting, and hence he is classed among the *Carnivora;* but when domesticated he will live upon vegetable substances alone, such as oatmeal porridge, or bread made from any of the cereals, but thrives best upon a mixed diet of vegetable and animal substances ; and, indeed, the formation of his teeth is such as to lead us to suppose that by nature he is intended for it, as we shall hereafter find in discussing his anatomical structure.

VARIETIES OF THE DOG.

The varieties of the dog are extremely numerous, and, indeed, as they are apparently produced by crossing, which is still had recourse to, there is scarcely any limit to the numbers which may be described. It is a curious fact that large bitches frequently take a fancy to dogs so small as to be incapable of breeding with them ; and in any case, if left to themselves, the chances are very great against their selecting mates of the same breed as themselves. The result is that innumerable nondescripts are yearly born, but as a certain number of breeds are described by writers on the dog, or defined by " dog-fanciers," these " mongrels," as they are called from not belonging to them, are generally despised, and however, useful they may be, the breed is not continued. This, however, is not literary true, exceptions being made in favor of certain sorts which have been improved by admixture with others, such as the cross of the bulldog with the greyhound ; the foxhound with the Spanish pointer ; the bulldog with the terrier, &c., &c., all of which are now recognized and admitted into the list of valuable breeds, and not only are not considered mongrels, but on the contrary, are prized above the original strains from which they are descended.

THE NORTH AND SOUTH AMERICAN DOGS.

A great variety of the dog tribe is to be met with throughout the continent of America, resembling in type the dingo of Australia, but appearing to be crossed with some of the different kinds introduced by Europeans. One of the most remarkable of the South American dogs is the *Alco*, which has pendulous ears, with a short tail and hog-back, and is supposed to be descended from the native dog found by Columbus ; but, even allowing this to be the case, it is of course much intermixed with foreign breeds. The North-American dogs are very closely allied to the dingo in all respects, but are generally smaller in size, and are also much crossed with European breeds. In some districts they burrow in the ground, but the march of civilization is yearly diminishing their numbers throughout the continent of America.

THE SMOOTH GREYHOUND.

This elegant animal appears to have existed in Britain from a very early period, being mentioned in a very old Welsh proverb, and a law of King Canute having precluded the commonalty from keeping him. Numberless hypotheses have been brought forward relative to the origin of the greyhound, Buffon tracing him to the French nation, and some other writers fancying that they could, with more probability, consider him as the descendant of the bulldog or the mastiff. But as I believe that it is impossible to ascertain with any degree of certainty the origin of the *species Canis*, so I am quite satisfied with the conclusion that no long-standing *variety* can be traced to its source. We must, therefore, be content to take each as we find it, and rest content with investigating its present condition ; perhaps in some cases extending our researches back for fifty or a hundred years, and even then we shall often find that we are lost in a sea of doubt.

Until within the last twenty-five years public coursing was confined to a very limited circle of competitors, partly owing to the careful retention of the best blood in the kennels of a chosen few, but chiefly to the existing game laws, which made it imperative that every person coursing should not only have a certificate, but also a qualification ; that is to say, the possession of landed property to the value of one hundred pounds per annum. Hence the sport was forbidden to the middle classes, and it was not until the passing of the present game laws, in 1831, that it was thrown open to them. From that time to the present the possession of the greyhound has been coveted and obtained by great numbers of country gentlemen and farmers in rural districts, and by professional men, as well as tradesmen, in our cities and towns, so that the total number in Great Britain and Ireland may be estimated at about fifteen or twenty thousand. Of these about five or six thousand are kept for public coursing, while the remainder amuse their owners by coursing the hare in private.

Various explanations have been offered of the etymology of the prefix *grey*, some contending that the color is implied, others that it means Greek (*Graius*), while a third party understand it to mean *great*. But as there is a remarkable peculiarity in this breed connected with it, we need not, I think, go farther for the derivation. No other breed, I believe, has the blue or grey color prevalent ; and those which possess it at all have it mixed with white, or other color ; as, for instance, the blue-bottled harrier, and the blotched blue and brown seen in some other kinds. The greyhound, on the contrary, has the pure blue or iron *grey* color very commonly ; and although this shade is not admired by any lovers of the animal for its beauty, it will make its appearance occasionally. Hence it may fairly be considered a peculiarity of the breed, and this grey color may, therefore, with a fair show of probability, have given the name to the greyhound.

The points of the greyhound will be described at length, because, as far as speed goes, he may be taken as the type to which all other breeds are referred ; but, before going into these particulars, it will be interesting to examine the oft-quoted doggrel rhymes, which are founded upon a longer effusion originally published by Wynkyn de Worde, in 1496, and to institute a comparison between the greyhound, of the fifteenth and nineteenth centuries. In the former of these periods it was said that this dog should have —

> " The head of a snake,
> The neck of the drake,
> A back like a beam,
> A side like a bream,
> The tail of a rat,
> And the foot of a cat.''

THE GAZEHOUND.

This breed is now lost, and it is very difficult to ascertain in what respects it differed from the greyhound. Bewick describes it minutely, but he does not appear to have any authority for what he writes on this particular.

THE ALBANIAN DOG.

The Albanian dog is said to stand about 27 or 28 inches high, with a long pointed muzzle, powerful body, strong and muscular limbs, and a long bushy tail, carried like that of the Newfoundland dog. His hair is very fine and close, being of a silky texture, and of a fawn color, variously clouded with brown. He is used for hunting the wild boar and wolf, as well as for the purpose of guarding the sheep-fold from the latter; but the accounts of this dog vary greatly, and are not much to be relied on.

THE ITALIAN GREYHOUND.

This little dog is one of the most beautifully proportioned animals in creation, being a smooth English greyhound in miniature, and resembling it in all respects but size. It is bred in Spain and Italy in great perfection, the warmth of the climate agreeing well with its habits and constitution. In England, as in its native country, it is only used as a pet or toy dog, for though its speed is considerable for its size, it is incapable of holding even a rabbit. The attempt, therefore, to course rabbits with this little dog has always failed, and in those instances where the sport (if such it can be called) has been carried out at all, recourse has been had to a cross between the Italian greyhound and the terrier, which results in a strong, quick, little dog, quite capable of doing all that is required.

The chief points characteristic of the Italian greyhound are shape, color, and size.

In *shape* he should as nearly as possible resemble the English greyhound. The nose is not usually so long in proportion, and the head is fuller both in width and depth. The eyes, also, are somewhat larger, being soft and full. The tail should be small in bone, and free from hair. It is scarcely so long as that of the English greyhound, bearing in mind the difference of size. It usually bends with a gentle sweep upwards, but should never turn round in a corkscrew form.

The *color* most prized is a golden fawn; the dove-colored fawn comes next; then the cream-color, and the blue fawn, or fawn with blue muzzle, the black-muzzled fawn, the black-muzzled red, the plain red, the yellow, the cream-colored, and the black ; the white, the blue, the white and fawn, and the white and red. Whenever the dog is of a whole color, there should be no white whatever on the toes, legs, or tail ; and even a star on the breast is considered a defect, though not so great as on the feet.

The *size* most prized is when the specified weight is about six or eight pounds ; but dogs of this weight have seldom perfect symmetry, and one with good shape and color of eight pounds is to be preferred to a smaller dog of less symmetry. Beyond 12 lbs. the dog is scarcely to be considered a pure Italian, though sometimes exceptions occur, and a puppy of pure blood, with a sire and dam of small size, may grow to such a weight as 16 lbs.

THE BLOODHOUND.

The name given to this hound is founded upon his peculiar power of scenting the blood of a wounded animal, so that, if once put on his trail, he could hunt him through any number of his fellows, and would thus single out a wounded deer from a large herd, and stick to him through any foils or artifices which he may have recourse to. From this property he has also been used to trace human beings, and as his nose is remarkably delicate in hunting, even without blood, he has always been selected for that purpose, whether the objects of pursuit were slaves, as in Cuba and America, or sheep-stealers as in England.

At present there are, as far as I know, no true bloodhounds in this country for this purpose, or indeed for any other, as I believe the breed to be extinct ; but several gentlemen possess hounds commonly called bloodhounds, though only partially resembling the veritable animal, and use them for hunting fallow-deer, especially those which are only wounded with the rifle, and not killed outright. This dog is also kept for his fine noble appearance, and as his temper is generally less uncertain than the genuine old bloodhound, and his taste for blood not so great, though still sometimes beyond all control, he is not unfitted to be the constant companion of man, but must always be regarded with some degree of suspicion.

THE FOX HOUND.

You desire to know what kind of hound I would recommend. As you mention not for any particular chase or country, I understand you generally ; and shall answer that I most approve of hounds of the middle size. I believe all animals of that description are strongest, and best able to endure fatigue. In the height as well as the color of hounds most sportsmen have their prejudices; but in their shape at least, I think they must all agree. I know sportsmen that boldly affirm that a small hound will oftentimes beat a large one; that he will climb hills better, and go through cover quicker; whilst others are not less ready to assert that a large hound will make his way in any country, will get better through the dirt than a small one, and that no fence, however high, can stop him. You have now their opinions, and I advise you to adopt that which suits your country best. There is, however, a certain size best adapted for business, which I take to be that between the two extremes, and I will venture to say that such hounds will not suffer themselves to be disgraced in any country. Somerville I find is of the same opinion.

THE TERRIER.

The terrier as used for hunting is a strong, useful little dog, with great endurance and courage, and with nearly as good a nose as the beagle or harrier. From his superior courage when crossed with the bulldog, as most vermin-terriers are, he has generally been kept for killing vermin whose bite would deter the spaniel or the beagle, but would only render the terrier more determined in his pursuit of them. Hence, he is the constant attendant on the rat-catcher, and is highly useful to the gamekeeper, as well as to the farmer who is annoyed with rats and mice. He is only kept for the purpose of destroying ground vermin, such as the rat or the weasel, or as a companion to man, for which purpose his fidelity and tractability make him peculiarly fitted. Terriers are now usually divided into four kinds: — 1st, The old English terrier; 2d, The Scotch (including the Dandie Dinmont); 3d, The Skye; and 4th, The modern toy dog.

The *English terrier* is a smooth-haired dog, weighing from about 6 to 10 lbs. His nose is very long and tapering neatly off, the jaw being slightly overhung, with a high forehead, narrow, flat skull, strong, muscular jaw, and small, bright eye, well set in the head; ears, when entire, are short and slightly raised, but not absolutely pricked, turning over soon after they leave the head. When cropped they stand up in a point, and rise much higher than they naturally would. The neck is strong, but of a good length; body very symmetrical, with powerful short loins, and chest deep rather than wide, Shoulders generally good, and very powerful, so as to enable the terrier to dig away at an earth for hours together without fatigue, but they must not be so wide as to prevent him from " going to ground." Fore legs straight and strong in muscle, but light in bone, and feet round and hare-like. Hind legs straight, but powerful. Tail fine, with a decided down carriage. The color of these dogs should be black and tan, which is the only true color, many are white, slightly marked with black, or sometimes, but very rarely blue. The true fox terrier was generally chosen with as much white as possible, so that he might be readily seen, either coming up after the pack, or when in the fox's earth, in almost complete darkness; but these were all crossed with the bull-dog. Those which are now kept for general purposes, are, however, most prized when of the black and tan color, and the more complete the contrast, that is, the richer the black and tan respectively, the more highly the dog is valued, especially if without any white. In most cases there is a small patch of tan over each eye; the nose and palate should always be black. Such is the pure English terrier, a totally different animal from the short, thick muzzled, spaniel-eyed, long-backed, cat-footed, curly-tailed abomination so prevalent in the present day. But he is a rank coward, unless crossed with the bulldog.

The *Scotch terrier* closely resembles the English dog in all but his coat, which is wiry and rough, and hence he is sometimes called the wire-haired terrier, a name perhaps better suited to a dog which has long been naturalized in England, and whose origin is obscure enough. Beyond this difference in externals, there is little to be said distinctive of the one from the other, the colors being the same, but white being more highly prized in the southern variety, and the black and tan when more or less mixed with grey, so as to give the dog a pepper and salt appearance, being characteristic of the true Scotch terrier; but there are numberless varieties in size, and also in shape and color. This is a very good vermin dog, and will hunt anything from a fox to a mouse; but while he may be induced to hunt feather, he never takes to it like fur, and prefers vermin to game at all times.

The *Dandie Dinmont* is represented by two colors of hair, which is sometimes rather hard, but not long; one entirely a reddish brown, and called the " mustard," the other grey or bluish grey on the back, and tan or light brown on the legs, and called the " pepper ;" both have the silky hair on the forehead. The legs are short, the body long, shoulder low, back slightly curved, head large, jaws long and tapered to the muzzle, which is not sharp; ears large and hanging close to the head, eyes full, bright and intelligent, tail straight and carried erect, with a slight curve over the back (houndlike); the weight 18 to 24 lbs., varying according to the strain, but the original Dandie was a heavy dog. Occasionally in a litter there may be some with the short folding ear of a bull-terrier, and also with some greater length of the legs; these are not approved of by fanciers, but nevertheless are pure, showing a tendency to cast back.

The *Skye terrier* is remarkable for his long weasel-shaped body, and for his short fin-like legs, added to which he has a long rather than a wide head, and also a neck of unusual dimensions, so that when measured from tip to tail the entire length is not more than three times his height. The nose is pointed, but so concealed in the long hair which falls over his eyes, that it is scarcely visible without a careful inspection; eyes keen and expressive, but small as compared with the

spaniel. The ears are long and slightly raised, but turning over ; tail
long, but small in bone and standing straight backwards, that is, not
curved over the back, but having only a very gentle sweep to prevent
touching the ground. Fore legs slightly bandy, yet this is not to be
sought for, but to be avoided as much as possible, though always more
or less present. The dew-claws are entirely absent, and if present may
be considered a mark of impurity. The colors most in request are
black, fawn, or blue, especially a dark slaty blue, and the slightest trace
of white is carefully avoided The hair is long and straight, hard and
not silky, parted down the back, and nearly reaching the ground on each
side, without the slightest curl or resemblence to wool. On the legs
and on the top of the head it is lighter in color than on the body, and is
softer and more silky. This dog is little used as a sporting or vermin
dog, being chiefly reserved for the companionship of man, but he is
sometimes employed as a vermin-killer, and is as game as the rest of the
terriers when employed for that purpose. His weight is from 10 to 18
lbs., averaging about 14. But the variations in this particular, as
indeed in almost all the points of the Skye terrier, are numerous beyond
description.

The *Maltese dog* is sometimes classed among the terriers, but, as it
has little affinity with them, it is included among the toy dogs.

The *Spanish pointer* is characterized by great height and weight,
large bones, and altogether heavy limbs, large and rather spreading feet,
and a small stern.

THE MODERN ENGLISH POINTER,

This is now one of the most beautiful of all sporting dogs, dividing
with the setter the admiration of all those who enjoy the pleasures
attending on the use of the gun.

The *points* desirable in the pointer are, a moderately large head, wide
rather than long, with a high forehead, and an intelligent eye of medium
size. Muzzle broad, with its outline square in front, not receding as in
'the hound. Flews manifestly present, but not pendent. The head
should be well set on the neck, with a peculiar form at the junction
only seen in the pointer. The neck itself should be long, convex in its
upper outline, without any tendency to dewlap or to a "ruff," as the
loose skin covered with long hair round the neck is called. The body
is of good length, with a strong loin, wide hips, and rather arched ribs,
the chest being well let down, but not in a hatchet shape as in the greyhound, and the depth of the *back ribs* being proportionally greater than
in that dog. The tail, or "stern," as it is technically called, is strong
at the root, but suddenly diminishing it becomes very fine, and then
continues nearly of the same size to within two inches of the tip, when
it goes off to a point looking as sharp as the sting of a wasp, and giving

the whole very much the appearance of that part of the insect, but magnified as a matter of course. This peculiar shape of the stern characterizes the breed, and its absence shows a cross with the hound, or some other dog.

THE PORTUGUESE POINTER

Resembles the Spanish in general form, but is furnished with a bushy stern, and looks like a cross with the old-fashioned spaniel.

THE DALMATIAN DOG.

The *Dalmatian dog* is a handsome, well-formed dog, standing about twenty-four or twenty-five inches high, and resembling the pointer in his shape, but usually having his ears cropped.

He is beautifully spotted with black on a white ground, and being remarkably fond of horses, and of road-work with them, he has long been employed in this country to accompany our carriages as an ornamental appendage; but this fashion has of late years subsided. Hence he is here commonly known as "the Coach Dog;" but in his native country he is used as a pointer in the field, and is said to perform his duties well enough.

THE SETTER (ENGLISH AND IRISH).

These dogs are commonly supposed to be the old spaniel, either crossed with the pointer or his setting powers educated by long attention to the breed.

THE RUSSIAN SETTER.

This dog was at one time, that is about twenty years ago, considered to be superior to our English breed, and many of them were then introduced into the kennels of our best sportsmen, but they are now almost lost sight of again.

THE SPANIEL.

The *Clumber spaniel*, which for a long time was confined to the Newcastle family, but has lately become very fashionable, is a remarkably low, long, and somewhat heavy dog. In weight he is from 30 to 40 lbs. Height 18 to 20 inches. The head is heavy, wide and full, the muzzle broad and square, generally of a flesh color.

The *cocker* can scarcely be minutely described, inasmuch as there are so many varieties in different parts of Great Britain.

The *Devonshire cocker* closely resembles the Welsh dog, both being of deep liver-color.

The *Welch cocker*, is one of the best of this division, being of good size, with strong loins, capital legs and feet, and an excellent nose. The coat is very slightly curled on the body, but the ears and legs are feathered, the tail being nearly bare of hair.   These dogs are still extensively used in Wales for the purpose of hunting the cocks, which are to be met with in the principality in large numbers during the season, and form one of the chief attractions to the shooter.

Water spaniels are commonly said to have web-feet, and this point is often made a ground of distinction from other dogs, but the fact is that all dogs have their toes united by membrane in the same way, the only distinction between the water and land dogs being that the former have larger feet, and that the membrane between the toes being more lax, they spread more in swimming, and are thus more useful in the water. Most people would understand, from the stress laid on web-feet in the water dogs, that the toes of the land dogs were nearly as much divided as those of man, but there are none so formed, and, as I before remarked, the toes of all are united throughout by a strong membrane.   The coat in all the water dogs is woolly and thickly matted, often curly, and in all more or less oily, so as to resist the action of the water.   This oil is rank in smell, and hence they are all unfit to be inmates of our houses, which is a strong objection to the poodle as a toy dog.

The *Irish water spaniel* consists of two distinct varieties, peculiar to the North and South of Ireland.   The *Northern* dog has short ears, with little feather either on them or on the legs, but with a considerable curl in his coat.   In color he is generally liver, but with more or less white, which sometimes predominates, so as to make him decidedly white and liver.   The *South country* Irish water spaniel is, on the contrary, invariably of a pure liver water color.   Ears long and well feathered, being often two feet from point to point, and the whole coat consisting of short crisp curls.   Body long, low, and strong, tail round and carried slightly down ; but straight, without any approach to feather.

The *poodle* was probably originally a water spaniel, but he is now used solely as a toy dog, in this country at all events.

THE ENGLISH SHEEP DOG.

This dog has a sharp muzzle, medium-sized head, with small and piercing eyes ; a well-shaped body, formed after the model of a strong low greyhound, but clothed in thick and somewhat woolly hair, which is particularly strong about the neck and bosom. The tail is naturally long and bushy, but, as it has almost invariably been cut off until of late years, its variations can hardly be known. Under the old excise laws, the shepherd's dog was only exempt from tax when without a tail, and for this reason it was always removed; from which at last it happened that many puppies of the breed were born without any tails, and to this day some particular breeds are tailless. In almost all sheep dogs there is a double dew-claw on each hind leg, and very often without any bony attachment. The legs and feet are strong and well formed, and stand road-work well, and the untiring nature of the dog is very remarkable. The color varies greatly, but most are grey, or black, or brown, with more or less white.

THE COLLEY.

One of the most beautiful and useful of all our dogs is the Scotch sheep-dog or colley. With a fine muzzle he combines an intelligent-looking and rather broad head, and a clear but mild eye, a pricked and small ear slightly falling at the tip. His body is elegantly formed, and clothed with a thick coat of woolly hair, which stands out evenly from his sides and protects him from all the vicissitudes of the weather, neither wind, rain, or snow being capable of penetrating it. The legs are well formed and the feet strong and useful. The tail is long, gently curved, and bushy, and the whole outline resembles the dingo; but the form is stouter and the limbs stronger. The color is nearly always black and tan, with little or no white; sometimes, however, the whole skin is one or other of these colors, but then the dog is not considered nearly so valuable. The colley, like the true English sheep-dog, has always one or two dew-claws on each hind foot. The sagacity and perseverance of this dog are wonderful, and the instances in which he has succeeded in saving sheep and lambs under perilous circumstances are beyond all description.

THE POMERANIAN WOLF-DOG.

This variety is used to protect the sheep from the wolf. His head is long, with a pointed muzzle, and short pricked ears. He is a large wolf-like dog in shape, with long silky hair on the body and tail, but short on the head, legs, and ears. The color is black, white, grey, or sometimes yellow. Tail long and spirally curled.

THE NEWFOUNDLAND.

This most valuable animal is of two very different kinds. viz., the large, loose-made, and long-haired variety, known as the Large Labrador ; and the small, compact, and comparatively short-haired dog, known as the St. John's, or Lesser Labrador breed. Both were originally natives of Newfoundland, and though many are bred in England, fresh specimens are constantly being imported from the island. All are now more or less crossed with the mastiff or setter. In this country they are chiefly used for ornamental purposes and as companions to their masters, the small breed being also crossed with the setter to make the retriever ; but in their native country they are used to draw timber over the snow in the winter months, being harnessed to carts and sledges made for the purpose. In intelligence the two breeds are about equal, both being celebrated for their faculty of learning to fetch and carry. This is sometimes developed to such an extent that a well-trained dog will go back for anything which his master has pointed out to him, if it has been handled. when it is only necessary to order him back to " seek," and he will find it by the scent. Many amusing instances of this are told, one of which we have heard on good authority, but which is almost beyond belief. A lady was most anxious to obtain a particular object from her lover, which he had strong reasons for refusing to her ; but being at length teased into complying he gave it to her, and after parting, at some distance from her home, he fetched his dog and ordered him to " go seek." The intelligent creature at once started off on the heel of his master, and, overtaking the lady still carrying the *gage d'amour*, he laid hold of it and brought it back in triumph. The dispossessed fair one, not having the least idea whose dog it was, and being ashamed to own how she had lost it, said nothing about the matter, and so the gentleman for once outwitted the lady in this stage of their courtship ; whether the tables were turned afterwards, and the dog was enlisted in her service, we know not. Both breeds are good water-dogs, and bear immersion for a long time. but the large variety having a more woolly coat is superior in endurance of wet and cold. Hundreds of anecdotes are told of extraordinary escapes from drowning by means of these dogs. their tendency to fetch and carry being doubly useful here. Children and light small women may be intrusted to them with safety in the water, if they are not bewildered with fear, when they will sometimes cling round the dog's neck, and frustrate all his efforts to restore them to the land by swimming ; generally, however, in cases of recovery, the person has fainted, and being then powerless is towed ashore readily enough. The speed with which the Newfoundland swims is very great, his large legs and feet enabling him to paddle himself with great force. From their great size and strength they are able to beat off most dogs when they are attacked, and their thick coats prevent the teeth of their assailants from doing much damage; but in offensive measures they are of little use, being rather unwieldy, and soon winded in a desperate struggle. Hence they are not useful in hunting the large kinds of game, nor the bear, wolf, or tiger. The nose is delicate enough to hunt any kind of scent, but as they soon tire they are not used in this way, and it is solely as retrievers on land or water that they are useful to the sportsman, being generally crossed with the setter for the former, and the water spaniel for the latter element.

The *characteristic points* of the Large Newfoundland are, great size, often being from thirty to thirty-two inches high; a form proportionally stout and strong, but loosely put together, so that there is a general want of compactness, especially about the loins, which are long and very flexible. The head is not large in comparison to the size, but wide across the eyes; muzzle of average length and width, and without any flews, as in the hounds and pointers; eye and ear both small, the latter falling, and without much hair on it; neck short and clothed with a ruff of hair; tail long, curled on itself slightly, and woolly; legs very strong, but not feathered; feet large and rather flat, bearing the road badly; coat on the body long, woolly, and matted; color black, or black and white, or white with little black, or liver color, or a reddish dun, or sometimes, but rarely, a dark brindle not very well marked.

The *St. John's*, or *Smaller Labrador*, or *Newfoundland*, the three names being used indiscriminately, is seldom more than twenty-five inches high, and often much less. The head is larger in proportion to his size, and the ear also slightly fuller; neck longer; body far more compact, and clothed with shorter hair, shining, and without any woolly texture; tail similar in shape, but the hair less woolly; legs and feet also better adapted for work; color almost always a jet black, rarely liver-colored.

THE ESQUIMAUX DOG.

This dog is the only beast of burden in the northern parts of the continent of America and adjacent islands; being sometimes employed to carry materials for hunting, or the produce of the chase, on his back; and at others he is harnessed to sledges in teams varying from seven to eleven, each being capable of drawing a hundred-weight for his share. They are harnessed to a single yoke-line by a breast-strap, and, being without any guide-reins, they are entirely at liberty to do what they like, being only restrained by the voice of their master, and urged forward by his whip. A single dog of tried intelligence and fidelity is placed as leader, and upon him the driver depends for his orders being obeyed. In the summer they are most of them turned off to get their own subsistence by hunting, some few being retained to carry weights on their backs; sledges are then rendered useless by the absence of snow; and, as there

2

is a good subsistence for them from the offal of the seal and the walrus which are taken by the men, the dogs become fat at this season of the year. The Siberian and Greenland dogs are nearly similar to those of Kamtschatka, but somewhat larger, and also more managable, all being used in the same way. The Esquimaux dog is about twenty-two or twenty-three inches high, with a pointed fox-like muzzle, wide head, pricked ears, and wolf-like aspect; the body is low and strong, and clothed with long hair, having an undercoat of thick wool; tail long, gently curved, and hairy; feet and legs strong and well formed; the color is almost always a dark dun with slight disposition to brindle, and black muzzle.

BULLDOG.

The *points* of a well-bred bulldog are as follows. The head should be round, the skull high, the eye of moderate size, and the forehead well sunk between the eyes, the ears semi-erect and small, well placed on the top of the head, rather close together than otherwise, the muzzle short, truncate, and well furnished with chop; his back should be short, well arched towards the stern, which should be fine and of moderate length; many bulldogs have what is called a crooked stern, as though the vertebræ of the tail were dislocated or broken. I am disposed to attribute this to in-breeding. The coat should be fine, though many superior strains are very woolly-coated; the chest should be deep and broad, the legs strong and muscular, and the foot narrow and well split up like a hare's.

THE MASTIFF.

The *English mastiff* is a fine noble-looking animal, and in temper is the most to be depended on of all the large and powerful dogs, being extremely docile and companionable, though possessed of the highest courage. When crossed with the Newfoundland or bloodhound, they answer well as yard-dogs, but the produce is generally of a savage nature, while the pure breed is of so noble and mild a nature that they will not on any provocation hurt a child or even a small dog, one of their most remarkable attributes being their fondness for affording protection.

The *points* of the mastiff are: — A head of large size between that of the bloodhound and bulldog in shape, having the volume of muscle of the latter, with the flews and muzzle of the former; the ear being of middle size but drooping, like that of the hound. The teeth generally meet, but if anything there is a slight protuberance of the lower jaw, never being uncovered by the upper lip like those of the bulldog. Eye small. In shape there is a considerable similarity to the hound, but much heavier in all its lines. Loin compact and powerful, and limbs strong. Tail very slightly rough, and carried high over the back when excited. Voice very deep and sonorous. Coat smooth. Color red or fawn with black muzzle, or brindled, or black; or black, red, or fawn and white. Height about twenty-five to twenty-eight inches; sometimes, but rarely, rather more.

THE MOUNT ST. BERNARD DOG.

Closely allied to the mastiff, but resembling the Newfoundland in temper and in his disposition to fetch and carry, is the Mount St. Bernard breed, confined to the Alps and the adjacent countries, where he is used to recover persons who are lost in the snow-storms of that inclement region. Wonderful stories are told of the intelligence of these dogs and of the recovery of travellers by their means, which are said to extend almost to the act of pouring spirits down the throats of their patients; but, however, there is no doubt that they have been and still are exceedingly useful, and the breed is still kept up at the monastery of Mount St. Bernard. The height is about twenty-five to twenty-eight inches; length six feet, including the tail. The coat is short but varies a good deal in length, and the color is a red or fawn with black muzzle, occasionally slightly marked in a brindled fashion. The shape of the head and body closely resembles that of the English mastiff, but rather heavier in all respects. Some dogs have been imported with decidedly rough coats.

THE POODLE.

This dog is generally to be seen shaved in part, so as to resemble the lion in having a mane, and the tip of his tail also having a tuft left on. He is by many supposed to be the produce of a cross between the water and land spaniels, but there is no good reason to suppose that the breed is not quite as distinct as either of them. For many years it has been known in France and Germany, particularly the former country, and it is there occasionally used for sporting purposes, though, as in England, it is chiefly as a companion that this dog is kept. With more intelligence than falls to the lot of any other dog, he unites great fidelity to his master, and a strong love of approbation, so that he may readily be induced to attempt any trick which is shown him, and the extent to which he may be taught to carry out the secret orders of his instructor is quite marvellous He fetches and carries very readily; swims well, and has a good nose, but has no particular fondness for hunting game, often preferring a stick or a stone to a hare or pheasant.

MALTESE DOG.

This beautiful little dog is a Skye terrier in miniature, with, however, a far more silky coat, a considerably shorter back, and a tail stiffly curved over the hip.

Points.—The weight should never exceed five or six pounds. Head closely resembling that of the Skye, but with more shining and silky hair. Coat as long as that dog's, but more transparent and silky. Actions lively and playful, and altogether rendering it a pleasing pet. The tail is curved over the back, very small and short, with a brush of silky hair. Color white, with an occasional patch of fawn on the ear or paw. The breed was so scarce some time ago as to induce Sir E. Landseer to paint one as the last of his race; since which several have been imported from Malta, and, though still scarce, they are now to be obtained.

THE LION DOG.

This toy dog appears to be a cross between the poodle and the Maltese dog, being curly like the former, but without his long ears and square visage. He is now very seldom seen in this country, and is not prized among fanciers of the canine species. Like the poodle he was generally shaved to make him resemble the lion.

THE KING CHARLES SPANIEL.

The *points* of the King Charles spaniel are : extremely short muzzle, which may be slightly turned up; black nose and palate; full, prominent eye, which is continually weeping, leaving a gutter of moisture down the cheek ; a round, bullet-shaped head ; very long, full-haired and silky ears, which should fall close to the cheeks, and not stand out from them. The body is covered with wavy hair of a silky texture, *without curl ;* and the legs should be feathered to the toes, the length and silkiness of this being a great point. Tail well feathered, but not bushy; it is usually cropped. The color should be a rich black and tan, without a white hair. The weight should never exceed 6, or at the utmost 7 lbs.; and they are valued the more if they are as low as $4\frac{1}{2}$ or 5 lbs.

THE PUG.

This curly and pretty little toy dog was out of fashion in England for some years, but has recently come again into such vogue that a good pug will fetch from 20 to 35 guineas. The British breed, however, which is one of those known to have existed from the earliest times, was never entirely lost, having been carefully preserved in a few families. The Dutch have always had a fondness for the pug dog, and in Holland the breed is common enough, but the same attention has not been paid to it as in England, and yellow masks, low foreheads and pointed noses are constantly making their appearance in them, from the impure blood creeping out and showing evidences of the crosses which have taken place. These dogs are not remarkable for sagacity displayed in any shape, but they are very affectionate and playful, and, like the Dutch and Flemish cows, they bear the confinement of the house better than many other breeds, racing over the carpets in their play as freely as others do over the turf. For this reason, as well as the sweetness of their skins, and their short and soft coats, they are much liked by the ladies as pets.

Their *points* are as follows :—General appearance low and thick-set, the legs being short, and the body as close to the ground as possible, but with an elegant outline. Weight from 6 to 10 lbs. Color fawn, with black mask and vent. The clearer the fawn, and the more distinctly marked the black on the mask, which should extend to the eyes, the better; but there is generally a slightly darker line down the back. Some strains have the hair all over the body tipped with "smut," but on them the mask is sure to shade off too gently, without the clear line which is valued by the fancier. Coat short, thick and silky. Head round, forehead high ; nose short, but not turned up ; and level-mouthed Ears always cropped close, naturally rather short but falling. Neck of moderate length, stout but not throaty. Chest wide, deep and round. Tail short, and curled clo ely to the side, not standing up above the back. It is remarkable that the tail in the dog generally falls over the off side, while in the bitch it lies on the near. The legs are straight, with small bone, but well clothed with muscle. Feet like the hare, not cat-footed. No dew-claws on the hind legs. The height is from 11 to 15 inches.

TOY TERRIERS.

These are of the various breeds described under the head of the terrier, but of smaller size than the average, and with great attention paid to their color and shape. The smooth English terrier, not exceeding 7 lbs. in weight, is much prized; and when he can be obtained of 3½ or 4 lbs. weight, with perfect symmetry, and a good rich black and tan color, without a white hair, he is certainly a very perfect little dog. Most of the toy terriers now sold are either crossed with the Italian greyhound or with the King Charles spaniel. If the former, the shape is preserved, and there is the greatest possible difficulty in distinguishing this cross from the pure English terrier; indeed, I am much inclined to believe that all our best modern toy terriers are thus bred. They have the beautiful long sharp nose, the narrow forehead, and the small sharp eye, which characterize the pure breed; but they are seldom good at vermin, though some which I have known to be half Italian have been bold enough to attack a good strong rat as well as most dogs. Many of these half-bred Italians are used for rabbit-coursing, in which there is a limit to weight, but it is chiefly for toy purposes that long prices are obtained for them. When the cross with the spaniel has been resorted to, the forehead is high, the nose short, and the eye large, full, and often weeping, while the general form is not so symmetrical and compact; the chest being full enough, but the brisket not so deep as in the true terrier or in the Italian cross.

The *Skye terrier*, as used for toy purposes, is often crossed with the spaniel to get silkiness of coat.

Scotch terriers are seldom used as toys, and are not considered such by the fanciers of the animal.

AXIOMS FOR THE BREEDER'S USE.

But it may be asked,—What then are the principles upon which breeding is to be conducted? To this, in many of the details, no answer can be given which can be relied on with certainty. Nevertheless, there are certain broad landmarks established which afford some assistance, and these shall be given, taking care to avoid all rules which are not clearly established by general consent.

1. The male and female each furnish their quota towards the original germ of the offspring; but the female over and above this nourishes it till it is born, and, consequently, may be supposed to have more influence upon its formation than the male.

2. Natural conformation is transmitted by both parents as a general law, and likewise any acquired or accidental variation. It may therefore be said that, on both sides, "*like produces like.*"

3. In proportion to the purity of the breed will it be transmitted unchanged to the offspring. Thus a greyhound bitch of pure blood put to a mongrel will produce puppies more nearly resembling her shape than that of the father.

4. Breeding in-and-in is not injurious to the dog, as may be proved both from theory and practice: indeed it appears, on the contrary, to be very advantageous in many well-marked instances of the greyhound, which have of late years appeared in public.

5. As every dog is a compound animal, made up of a sire and dam, and also their sires and dams, &c., so, unless there is much breeding in-

and-in, it may be said that it is impossible to foretell with absolute certainty what particular result will be elicited.

6. The first impregnation appears to produce some effect upon the next and subsequent ones. It is therefore necessary to take care that the effect of the cross in question is not neutralized by a prior and bad impregnation. This fact has been so fully established by Sir John Sebright and others that it is needless to go into its proofs

By these general laws on the subject of breeding we must be guided in the selection of the dog and bitch from which a litter is to be obtained, always taking care that both are as far as possible remarkable, not only for the bodily shape, but for the qualities of the brain and nervous system which are desired. Thus, in breeding the pointer, select a good looking sire and dam by all means, but also take care that they were good in the field; that is, that they possessed good noses, worked well, were stout, and if they were also perfectly broken so much the better. So, again, in breeding hounds, care must be taken that the animals chosen are shaped as a hound should be; but they should also have as many of the good hunting qualities, and as few of the vices of that kind of dog; and if these points are not attended to the result is not often good.

To secure these several results *the pedigrees* of the dog and bitch are carefully scanned by those who are particular in these matters, because then assurance is given that the ancestors, as far as they can be traced, possessed all those qualifications without which their owners would not in all human probability retain them. Hence a pointer, if proved to be descended from a dog and bitch belonging to Lord Sefton, Lord Lichfield, or any well-known breeder of this dog in the present day, or from Sir H. Goodrich, Mr. Moore, or Mr. Edge, so celebrated for their breeds some years ago, would be valued more highly than another without any pedigree at all, although the latter might be superior in shape, and might perform equally well in the field. The importance of pedigree is becoming more fully recognized every year, and experienced breeders generally refuse to have anything to do with either dog or bitch for this particular purpose, unless they can trace the pedigree to ancestors belonging to parties *who were known to be themselves careful in their selections.* In most cases this is all that is attempted, especially in pointers, setters, spaniels, &c., but in greyhounds and foxhounds of first-class blood the genealogy may generally be traced through half a dozen kennels of known and established reputation; and this same attention to breed ought to prevail in all the varieties of the dog whose performances are of importance, and indeed without it the reproduction of a particular shape and make cannot with anything like certainty be depended on. Hence the breeders of valuable toy dogs, such as King Charles spaniels, Italian greyhounds, &c., are as careful as they need be, having found out by experience that without this attention they are constantly disappointed.

IMPORTANCE OF HEALTH IN BOTH SIRE AND DAM.

Health in both parents should be 'especially insisted upon, and in the bitch in particular there should be a sufficiently strong constitution, to enable her to sustain the growth of her puppies before birth, and to produce milk enough for them afterwards, though in this last particular she may of course be assisted by a foster-nurse.

BEST AGE TO BREED FROM.

The best age to breed from, in almost all breeds, is soon after the sire and dam have each reached maturity. When, however, the produce is desired to be very small, the older both animals are, the more likely this result is, — excepting in the last litter which the bitch has, for this being often composed of only one or two puppies, they are not smaller than the average, and sometimes even larger. All bitches should be allowed to reach full maturity before they are allowed to breed, and this period varies according to size, small dogs being adult at one year, whereas large ones are still in their puppyhood at that time, and take fully twice as long to develop their proportions. The mastiff is barely full grown at two years ; large hounds at a year and a half ; greyhounds at the same time ; pointers and setters from a year and a quarter to a year and a half ; while terriers and small toy dogs reach maturity at a year old, or even earlier.

DURATION OF HEAT.

The duration of the period of heat in the bitch is about three weeks, during the middle week of which she will generally take the dog ; but about the eleventh or twelfth day from the first commencement, is, on the average, the best time to put her to him. During the first three or four days of the middle week the bitch " bleeds " considerably from the *vulva,* and while this is going on she should not be allowed access to the male, nor will she generally if left to herself, but as soon as it subsides, no time should be lost, as it often happens that very shortly afterwards she will refuse him altogether, and thus a whole year may be lost. Most bitches are " in heat " twice a year, at equal periods, some every five, or even every four, months ; others every seven, eight, nine, ten, eleven, or twelve months ; but the far greater proportion of bitches of all breeds are " in season " twice a year pretty regularly. There is, therefore, a necessity for ascertaining the rule in each bitch, as it varies so considerably ; for, when it is known, the calculation can better be made as to the probability of the heat returning at the desired time. The period between the first and second "heats" will generally indicate the length of the succeeding ones, but this is not invariable, as the "putting by" of the animal will sometimes throw her out of her regular course.

MANAGEMENT OF THE BITCH IN WHELP.

When it is clearly ascertained that the bitch is in whelp, the exercise should be increased and carried on freely till the sixth week, after which it should be daily given, but with care to avoid strains either in galloping or jumping. A valuable bitch is often led during the last week, but somehow or other she ought to have walking exercise to the last, by which in great measure all necessity for opening medicine will be avoided. During the last few weeks her food should be regulated by her condition, which must be raised if she is too low, or the reverse if she is too fat, the desired medium being such a state as is compatible with high health, and neither tending towards exhaustion nor inflammation. Excessive fat in a bitch not only interferes with the birth of the pups, but also is very liable to interfere with the secretion of milk, and, if this last does happen, aggravates the attendant or "milk" fever. To know by the eye and hand how to fix upon this proper standard, it is only necessary to feel the ribs, when they should at once be apparent to the hand, rolling loosely under it, but not evident to the eye so as to count them. It is better to separate the bitch from other dogs during the last week or ten days, as she then becomes restless, and is instinctively and constantly looking for a place to whelp in, whereas, if she is prevented from occupying any desirable corner she is uneasy. At this time the food should be of a very sloppy nature, chiefly composed of broth, or milk and bread, adding oatmeal according to the state of the bowels.

PREPARATION FOR WHELPING.

' The best mode of preparing a place for the bitch to whelp in is to nail a piece of old carpet over a smooth boarded floor, to a regular "bench," if in a sporting kennel ; or on a door or other flat piece of board raised a few inches from the ground, if for any other breed. When a regular wooden box or kennel, as these are called in ordinary language, is used for the bitch, she may as well continue to occupy it, as she will be more contented than in a fresh place ; but it is not so easy to get at her there if anything goes wrong with either mother or whelps, and on that account it is not a desirable place. A board, large or small, according to the size of the bitch, with a raised edge to prevent the puppies rolling off, and supported by bricks a few inches from the ground, is all that is required for the most valuable animal ; and if a piece of carpet, as before mentioned, is tacked upon this, and some straw placed upon all, the height of comfort is afforded to both mother and offspring. The use of the carpet is to allow the puppies to catch their claws in it as they are working at the mother's teats ; for without it they slip over the board, and they are restless, and unable to fill themselves well ; while at the same time they scratch all the straw away, and are left bare and cold.

DESTRUCTION OR CHOICE OF WHELPS AT BIRTH.

Sometimes it is desirable to destroy all the whelps as soon as possible after birth, but this ought very seldom to be done, as in all cases it is better to keep one or two sucking for a short time, to prevent milk fever, and from motives of humanity also. If, however, it is decided to destroy all at once, take them away as fast as they are born, leaving only one with the mother to engage her attention, and when all are born, remove the last before she has become used to it, by which plan less cruelty is practised than if she is permitted to attach herself to her offspring. Low diet and a dose or two of mild aperient medicine, with moderate exercise, will be required to guard against fever, but at best it is a bad business, and can only be justified under extraordinary circumstances.

CHOICE OF WHELPS.

To choose the whelps in the nest which are to be kept, most people select on different principles, each having some peculiar crotchet to guide himself. Some take the heaviest, some the last born ; others the longest of the litter ; while others again are entirely guided by color. In toy dogs, and those whose appearance is an important element, color ought to be allowed all the weight it deserves, and among certain toy dogs the value is often affected a hundred per cent. by a slight variation in the markings.

FEEDING BEFORE WEANING.

The food of whelps before weaning should be confined at first to cow's milk, or, if this is very rich, reduced with a little water. It is better to boil it, and it should be sweetened with fine sugar, as for the human palate. As much of this as the whelps will take may be given them three times a day, or every four hours if they are a large litter. In the fourth week get a sheep's head, boil it in a quart of water till the meat comes completely to pieces, then carefully take away every particle of bone, and break up the meat into fragments no larger than a small horse-bean; mix all up with the broth, thicken this to the consistence of cream with *fine* wheat flour, boil for a quarter of an hour, then cool and give alternately with the milk. At this time the milk may also be thickened with flour; and as the puppies grow, and the milk of the bitch decreases in quantity, the amount of milk and thickened broth must be increased each day, as well as more frequently given. Some art, founded on experience, is required; not to satiate the puppies, but by carefully increasing the quantity whenever the pups have finished it greedily the last time or two, they will not be overdone. In no case should the pan containing the food be left in the intervals with the puppies, if they have not cleared it out, as they only become disgusted with it, and next time refuse to feed. A sheep's head will serve a litter of large-sized puppies two days up to weaning, more or less according to numbers and age.

WEANING.

When weaning is to be commenced, which is usually about the 5th or 6th week, it is better to remove the puppies altogether, than to let the bitch go on suckling them at long intervals. By this time their claws and teeth have become so sharp and so long, that they punish the bitch terribly, and therefore she does not let them fill their bellies. Her milk generally accumulates in her teats, and becomes stale, in which state it is not fit for the whelps, and by many is supposed to engender worms. The puppies have always learned to lap, and will eat meat, or take broth or thickened milk, as described in the last chapter; besides which, when they have no chance of sucking presented to them, they take other food better, whereas, if they are allowed to suck away at empty teats, they only fill themselves with wind, and then lose their appetites for food of any kind. But, having determined to wean them, there are several important particulars which must be attended to, or the result will be a failure, at all events for some time. That is to say, the puppies will fall away in flesh, and will cease to grow at the same rate as before. In almost all cases, what is called the " milk-fat " disappears after weaning, but still it is desirable to keep some flesh on their bones, and this can only be done by attending to the following directions, which apply to dogs of all kinds, but are seldom rigidly carried out, except with the greyhound, whose size and strength are so important as to call for every care to procure them in a high degree. In hounds, as well as pointers and setters, a check in the growth is of just as much consequence; but as they are not tested together as to their speed and stoutness so closely as greyhounds are, the slight defects produced in puppy-hood are not detected, and, as a consequence, the same attention is not paid. Nevertheless, as most of these points require only care, and cost little beyond it, they ought to be carried out almost as strictly in the kennels of the foxhound and pointer as in those devoted to the longtails. These chief and cardinal elements of success are,—1st, a warm, clean and dry lodging; 2dly, suitable food; 3dly, regularity in feeding; and 4tbly, a provision for sufficient exercise.

THE USE OF THE DOG IN SHOOTING.

The dogs used in aid of the gun are : the pointer, the setter, in grouse and partridge shooting; the spaniel, beagle, and terrier, in covert shooting; either of the above in snipe shooting; and the water spaniel or retriever in wild fowl shooting.

TEETH OF THE DOG AT VARIOUS AGES.

The *incisors* are somewhat remarkable in shape, having three little lobules at their edges resembling a *fleur-de-lis*. Next to these come the canine teeth or tusks, and then the molars, which vary in form considerably. In the upper jaw, in front, are three sharp and cutting teeth, which Cuvier calls *false* molars; then a tooth with two cutting lobes; and lastly two flat teeth, or *true* molars. In the under jaw, the first four molars on each side are *false*, or cutters; then an intermediate one, with the posterior part flat; and lastly two tubercular teeth, or true molars. As the incisors are worn away and the dog becomes old, the lobules on the edges wear away and are flattened. The teeth are developed in two sets : the first, called *milk-teeth*, showing themselves through the gums about a fortnight or three weeks after birth, and lasting till the fifth or sixth month, when they are displaced by the *permanent set*, the growth of which is accompanied by a degree of feverishness which is often mistaken for distemper. The dog's teeth should be beautifully white, if he is healthy and well reared, and until the third year there should be no deposit of tartar upon them, but after that time they are always coated with this substance at the roots, more or less, according to the feeding and state of health.

THE MUSCULAR SYSTEM.

The *muscles* of the dog have nothing remarkable about them, excepting that they are renewed and wasted faster than in most animals. This has passed into a proverb, and should be known as influencing the time which dogs take to recruit their strength.

THE BRAIN AND NERVOUS SYSTEM.

The *nervous system* is highly developed in those breeds which have been carefully attended to, that is, where individuals of high nervous sensibility have been selected to breed from. This is therefore remarkable in the bulldog, selected for generations for courage ; in the pointer, where steadiness in pointing has been the prominent cause of choice ; and in the greyhound, whose characteristic is speed ; all requiring a high development of the nervous system, and all particularly liable to nervous diseases, such as fits, chorea, &c. On the other hand, the cur, the common sheep-dog, &c., seldom suffer from any disease whatever.

THE DIGESTIVE SYSTEM.

The *stomach* of this animal is extremely powerful in dissolving bones, but it is also very liable to sickness, and on the slightest disturbance rejects its contents. This appears to be almost a natural effect, and not a diseased or disordered condition, as there is scarcely a dog which does not wilfully produce vomiting occasionally by swallowing grass. Few medicines which are at all irritating will remain down, and a vast number which are supposed to be given are not retained on the stomach, while others are only partially so. The bowels are extremely liable to become costive, which is in great measure owing to the want of proper exercise, and this also is very apt to produce torpidity of the liver. It may, however, be observed that in almost all particulars, except the tendency to vomit, the digestive organs of the dog resemble those of man.

THE SKIN.

The skin of the dog is said to be quite free from perspiration, but this is a mistake, as I have often seen the short hairs of a smooth-coated dog glistening with fine beads of liquid, poured out on a hot day, when strong exercise was taken. The tongue, however, is the grand means of carrying off heat by evaporation, and its extensive surface, when hanging out of the mouth, is sufficient for the purpose, as the fluid is carried off more rapidly from the air passing over it in expiration. I am persuaded that a considerable amount of insensible perspiration is constantly going on from the surface of the skin, and that nothing ought to be done which is likely to check it. This, however, is contrary to the generally received opinion, which is that nothing of the kind takes place in this animal.

ADMINISTRATION OF REMEDIES.

Some considerable tact and knowledge of the animal are required in order to give medicines to the dog to the best advantage. In the first place, his stomach is peculiarly irritable, and so much under the control of the will, that most dogs can vomit whenever they like. Hence it is not only necessary to give the medicine, but also to insure its being kept down. For this purpose, however, it is generally only necessary to keep up the dog's head, as he will not readily vomit withot bringing his nose to the ground, and so it is the regular practice in large kennels, in giving a dose of physic, to put the couples on, and fasten them up to a hook, at such a height that the dog cannot lower his head, maintaining this position for two or three hours. A single dog may be watched, if such is preferred, but a lot of hounds in physic must be treated with less ceremony.

MODE OF GIVING A BOLUS OR PILL.

If the dog is small, take him on the lap, without harshness, and if inclined to use his paws tie a coarse towel round his neck, letting it fall down in front, which will muffle them effectually : then with the finger and thumb of the left hand press open the mouth by insinuating them between the teeth, far enough back to take in the cheeks, and so to compel the mouth to open from the pain given by the pressure against the teeth, while it also prevents the dog from biting the fingers. Then raising the nose, drop the pill as far back as possible, and push it well down the throat with the forefinger of the right hand. Let go with the left, still hold the nose up, keeping the mouth shut, and the pill is sure to go down. A large dog requires two persons to give a pill, if he is at all inclined to resist. First, back him into a corner, then stride over him, and putting a thick cloth into his mouth, bring it together over the nose, where it is held by the left hand ; the right can then generally lay hold of the lower jaw. But if the dog is very obstinate and inclined to resist, another cloth must also be placed over that, and then drawing them apart an assistant can push the pill down. Very often a piece of meat may be used to wrap the pill up in, and the dog will readily bolt it ; but sometimes it is desirable to avoid this, as it may be necessary to give the medicine by itself. Even large dogs, however, are seldom so troublesome as to require the above precautions in giving pills, though they almost always obstinately refuse liquid medicine when they have tasted it once or twice.

MODE OF DRENCHING THE DOG.

If a small quantity only is to be given, the dog's head being held, the liquid may be poured through the closed teeth, by making a little pouch of the cheek; but this is a tedious process, as the animal often refuses to swallow it for a long time, and then struggles till half is wasted. A spoon answers for small quantities, but for larger a soda-water bottle is the best instrument. Then, having the dog held on either of the plans recommended in the last paragraph, pour a little down, and shut the mouth, which is necessary, because the act of swallowing cannot be performed with it open. Repeat this till all is swallowed. Then watch the dog, or tie his head up, till it is clear that the medicine will be retained on the stomach.

THE APPLICATION OF THE MUZZLE.

When any operation is to be performed which is likely to make the dog use his teeth, he must be muzzled, either with an instrument made on purpose, or with a piece of tape, which is to be first wound round the nose of the dog, as close to the eyes as possible without touching them, then tied in a knot between them, and both ends brought back over the forehead to the collar, where they are to be made fast. When a muzzle is required to be worn by a savage dog, either in-doors or out, it must be so made as to allow of his readily putting his tongue out. For this purpose either a cone of leather pierced with holes, or of wire, is strapped on by a neck-strap and two or three side-straps.

FEVERS.

The dog is peculiarly liable to febrile attacks, which have always a tendency to put on a low form, very similar in its nature to that known as typhus in human medicine. This is so generally the case, that every dog is said to have the distemper at some time of his life, that name being given to this low form of fever. Hence, an attack may commence with a common cold, or any inflammatory affection of the lungs, bowels, &c.; but, this going on to assume the low form, it becomes a case of genuine typhus fever, or distemper. Nevertheless, it does not follow that the one must necessarily end in the other; and so the dog may have simple fever, known as "a cold," or various other complaints, without being subjected to the true distemper. The fevers occuring in the dog are: 1st, Simple ephemeral fever, commonly called "a cold;" 2nd, Simple epidemic fever, or influenza; 3rd, Typhus fever, known as Distemper; 4th, Rheumatic fever, attacking the muscular and fibrous systems; and, 5thly, Small-pox.

SIMPLE EPHEMERAL FEVER.

Symptoms.—This slight disease, known as "a common cold," is ushered in by chilliness, with increased heat of surface, a quick pulse, and slightly hurried breathing. The appetite is not as good as usual, eyes look dull, bowels costive, urine scanty and high-colored. There are often cough and slight running at the nose and eyes, and sometimes the other internal organs are attacked; or the disease goes on till a different form of fever is established, known as typhus, and this is particularly the case when many dogs are collected together, or when one or two are kept in a close kennel, and are neither properly ventilated nor cleaned.

INFLUENZA.

The Symptoms of influenza at first closely resemble those of the last-described attack, but as they depend upon some peculiar condition of the air which prevails at the time, and as they are more persistent, the name influenza is given. After the first few days the running at the eyes and nose increases, and a cough is almost always present, which symptoms often persist for two or three weeks, leaving great prostration of strength at the end of that time, and often a chronic cough, which requires careful treatment.

TYPHUS FEVER, OR DISTEMPER.

The *symptoms* are very various, but they may be divided into two sets, one of which comprises a set always attending upon distemper; while the other may or may not be present in any individual attack. The *invariable* symptoms are: a low, insidious fever, with prostration of strength to a remarkable degree, in proportion to the duration and strength of the attack, and rapid emaciation, so that a thick, muscular dog is often made quite thin and lanky in three days. As a part of the fever, there is shivering, attended by quick pulse, hurried respiration, loss of appetite, and impaired secretions; but, beyond these three, are no signs which can be called positively invariable; though the running at the eyes and nose, and the short husky cough, especially after exercise, are very nearly always present. The *accidental* symptoms depend upon the particular complication which may exist; for one of the most remarkable features in distemper is, that, coupled with the above invariable symptoms, there may be congestion, or inflammation of the head, chest, bowels, or skin. So that in one case the disease may appear to be entirely confined to the head, in another to the chest, and in a third to the bowels; yet all are strictly from the same cause, and require the same general plan of treatment, modified according to the seat of the complication.

The ordinary course of an attack of distemper is as follows: that is, when contracted by contagion, or clearly epidemic. (On the other hand, when it is developed in consequence of neglect, it comes on at the end of some other attack of disease, which may have existed for an indefinite time.) Almost always the first thing noticed is a general dulness or lassitude, together with loss of appetite. In a day or two there is generally a peculiar husky cough, which sounds as if the dog were trying to get a piece of straw out of his throat, and always comes on at exercise after a gallop. With this there is also a tendency to sneeze, but not so marked as the "husk" or "tissuck" which *may* occur in common "cold" or influenza, but is then usually more severe, and also more variable in its severity; soon going on to inflammation, or else entirely ceasing in a few days. In distemper, the strength and flesh rapidly fail and waste, while in common "cold" the cough may continue for days without much alteration in either; and this is one of the chief characteristics of the true disease. There is, also, generally a black, pitchy condition of the *fæces*, and the urine is scanty and high-colored. The white of the eyes is always more or less reddened, the color being of a bluish red cast, and the vessels being evidently gorged with blood. When the brain is attacked, the eyes are more injected than when the bowels or lungs are the seats of complication. The corners of the eyes have a small drop of mucus, and the nose runs more or less, which symptoms, as the disease goes on, are much aggravated, both being glued up by brownish matter, while the teeth also are covered with a blackish brown fur. Such are the regular symptoms of a severe attack of distemper, gradually increasing in severity to the third, fourth, or fifth week, when the dog dies from exhaustion, or from disease of the brain, lungs, or bowels, marked by peculiar signs in each case. In this course the disease may be described as passing through four *stages* or *periods:* 1st, that in which the poison is spreading through the system, called *the period of incubation;* 2nd, that in which nature rouses her powers to expel it, called *the period of reaction;* 3rd, *the period of prostration,* during which the powers of nature are exhausted, or nearly so, by the efforts which have been made; and 4th, *the period of convalescence.* On the average, each of these will occupy a week or ten days, varying with the mildness or severity of the attack.

When the head is attacked, there may or may not be a running from the nose and eyes; but more usually there is some evidence of congestion in these organs, the eyes being weak and glued up with the mucus, and the nose running more or less. A fit is, however, the clearest evidence of brain affection, and, to a common observer, the only reliable one. Sometimes there is stupor without a fit, gradually increasing till the dog becomes insensible and dies. At others, a raving delirium comes on, easily mistaken for hydrophobia, but distinguished from it by the presence of the premonitory symptoms peculiar to distemper. This

3

is the most fatal complication of all, and, if the dog recovers, he is often
a victim to palsy or chorea for the rest of his life.

If the lungs are attacked, there is very rapid breathing, with cough,
and almost always a considerable running from the eyes and nose, and
expectoration of thick, frothy mucus. If inflammation of the lungs is
established, the danger is as great as when the head is the seat of the
seizure.

The bowels may be known to be seized when there is a violent purg-
ing of black offensive matter, often tinged with blood, and sometimes
mixed with patches or shreds of a white leathery substance, which is
coagulable lymph. The discharge of blood is in some cases excessive,
and rapidly carries off the dog.

If the skin is attacked, which is a favorable sign, there is a breaking
out of pustules on the inside of the thighs and belly, which fill with matter often tinged with dark blood, and sometimes with blood itself of a
dark purple color.

To distinguish distemper from similar affections is not always easy
to an inexperienced observer, but the practised eye at once detects the
difference. The chief diseases which are likely to be confounded with
it are, the true canine madness, common "cold," or influenza, inflammation of the lungs, and diarrhœa. The first of these runs a more
rapid course, and is ushered in by peculiar changes in the temper, which
will be described under the head of HYDROPHOBIA. "Cold" and influenza cause no great prostration of strength; and the former comes on
after exposure to the weather, while the latter is sure to be prevalent at
the time. Inflammation of the lungs must be studied to be known,
and simple diarrhœa has no fever attending upon it.

RHEUMATIC FEVER.

One of the most common diseases in the dog is rheumatism in some
form, generally showing itself with very little fever, but sometimes
being accompanied with a high degree of that attendant evil. The
frequency of this disease is owing to the constant exposure of the dog to
cold and wet, and very often to his kennel being damp, which is the
fertile source of kennel lameness, or chest-founder, which is nothing
more than rheumatism of the muscles of the shoulders. Again, those
which spend half their time before a roasting fire, and the other half in
the wet and cold, are extremely apt to contract this kind of fever, but
not in so intractable a form as the denizen of the damp kennel. By
some writers this affection is classed among the inflammations; and it
is a debatable point to which of these divisions it should be assigned;
but this is of little consequence, so that it is properly known and easily
recognized by the symptoms. I shall therefore include here rheumatic
fever, which is a general affection, and also the partial attacks known
as kennel lameness or chest-founder, and rheumatism of the loins, commonly called palsy of the back.

Rheumatic fever is known by the following signs :—There is considerable evidence of the fever, but not of a very high character, the pulse being full but not very quick, with shivering and dulness, except when touched or threatened, the slighest approach causing a shriek, evidently from the fear of pain.   The dog almost always retires into a corner, and is very reluctant to come out of it.   On being forcibly brought out, he snarls at the hand even of his best friend, and stands with his back up, evidently prepared to defend himself from the pat of the hand, which to him is anguish.   The bowels are confined, and the urine high-coloured and scanty.

A dragging of the hind limbs is common enough in the dog, and, though often called palsy, it really is almost always of a rheumatic nature.   It exactly resembles chest-founder in all its symptoms, excepting that the muscles affected are situated in the loins and hips, corresponding with the human lumbago in all its particulars, excepting that it is far more permanent.   The *causes* and *treatment* are the same as those of kennel lameness.

SYMPATHETIC FEVER.

This term is applied to the fever which comes on either before or after some severe local affection, and being, as it were, eclipsed by it. Thus in all severe inflammations there is an accompanying fever which generally shows itself before the exact nature of the attack is made manifest, and though it runs high, yet it has no tendency in itself to produce fatal results, subsiding, as a matter of course, with the inflammation which attends it.   The same happens in severe injuries ; but here also, if there is no inflammation, there is no fever ; so that the same rule applies as where there is an external cause.

HYDROPHOBIA, RABIES, OR MADNESS.

This disease has been classed among the inflammations, although it has not been proved to arise from that cause ; but, as it is generally supposed to be connected with an inflammation or congestion of the spinal column or brain, there is every reason for placing it at the head of this division ; and, as it is of the utmost importance to understand its symptoms, the sooner it is studied the better.   At present there appears to be little or no control over this horrible complaint, so that it is solely with a view to recognize the attack and prevent its transmission by inoculation, that it is interesting to the owner of the dog.

The *symptoms* are chiefly as follows : — The first is a marked change of temper ; the naturally cheerful dog becoming waspish and morose, and the bold fondling pet retreating from his master's hand as if it was that of a stranger. On the other hand, the shy dog becomes bold; but in almost every case there is a total change of manner for several days before the absolute outbreak of the attack, which is indicated by a kind of delirious watching of imaginary objects, the dog snapping at the wall, or, if anything comes in his way, tearing it to pieces with savage fury. With this there is constant watchfulness, and sometimes a peculiarly hollow howl, while at others no sound whatever is given, the case being then described as "dumb madness." ' Fever is always present, but it is difficult to ascertain its extent on account of the danger of approaching the patient, and with this (in contradiction to the name hydrophobia), there is invariably an urgent thirst, which the dog is in such a hurry to gratify that he generally upsets the vessel containing his water. Mr. Grantley Berkeley maintains very strongly that no dog really attacked with rabies will touch water, and that the presence of thirst is a clear sign of the absence of this disease; but this opinion is so entirely in opposition to the careful accounts given by all those who have witnessed the disease when it had unquestionably been communicated either to man or to some of the lower animals, that no reliance ought to be placed upon it, especially where so important a stake is involved. Mr. Youatt witnessed more cases of rabies than perhaps any equally good observer ever did, and he strongly insists upon the presence of thirst, as may be gathered from the concluding portion of the following extract : —

" Some very important conclusions may be drawn from the appearance and character of the urine. The dog, and at particular times when he is more than usually salacious, may, and · does diligently search the urining places; he may even, at those periods, be seen to lick the spot which another has just wetted; but, if a peculiar eagerness accompanies this strange employment, if, in the parlor, which is rarely disgraced by this evacuation, every corner is perseveringly examined, and licked with unwearied and unceasing industry, that dog cannot be too carefully watched, there is great danger about him; he may, without any other symptom, be pronounced to be decidedly rabid. I never knew a single mistake about this.

" Much has been said of the profuse discharge of saliva from the mouth of the rabid dog. It is an undoubted fact that, in this disease, all the glands concerned in the secretion of saliva, become increased in bulk and vascularity. The sublingual glands wear an evident character of inflammation ;' but it never equals the increased discharge that accompanies epilepsy or nausea. The frothy spume at the corners of the mouth is not for a moment to be compared with that which is evident enough in both of these affections. It is a symptom of short duration, and seldom lasts longer than two hours. The stories that are told of the mad dog covered with froth are altogether fabulous. The dog recovering from, or attacked by, a fit may be seen in this state; but not the rabid dog. Fits are often mistaken for rabies, and hence the delusion.

"The increased secretion of saliva soon passes away. It lessens in quantity ; it becomes thicker, viscid, adhesive, and glutinous. It clings to the corners of the mouth, and probably more annoyingly so to the membrane of the fauces. The human being is sadly distressed by it, he forces it out with the greatest violence, or utters the falsely supposed bark of a dog, in his attempts to force it from his mouth. This symptom occurs in the human being when the disease is fully established, or at a late period of it. The dog furiously attempts to detach it with his paws.

"It is an early symptom in the dog, and it can scarcely be mistaken in him. When he is fighting with his paws at the corners of his mouth, let no one suppose that a bone is sticking between the poor fellow's teeth ; nor should any useless and dangerous effort be made to relieve him. If all this uneasiness arose from a bone in the mouth, the mouth would continue permanently open, instead of closing when the animal for a moment discontinues his efforts. If after a while he loses his balance and tumbles over, there can be no longer any mistake. It is the saliva becoming more and more glutinous, irritating the fauces and threatening suffocation.

"*To this naturally and rapidly succeeds an insatiable thirst.* The dog that still has full power over the muscles of his jaws continues to lap. He knows not when to cease, while the poor fellow laboring under the dumb madness, presently to be described, and whose jaw and tongue are paralysed, plunges his muzzle into the water-dish to his very eyes, in order that he may get one drop of water into the back part of his mouth to moisten and to cool his dry and parched fauces. Hence, instead of this disease being always characterized by the dread of water in the dog, it is marked by a thirst often perfectly unquenchable. Twenty years ago this assertion would have been peremptorily denied. Even at the present day, we occasionally meet with those who ought to know better, and who will not believe that the dog which fairly, or perhaps eagerly, drinks, can be rabid."—*Youatt*, pp. 135-6.

From my own experience I can fully confirm the above account, having seen seven cases of genuine rabies, in all of which thirst was present in a greater or less degree ; and in five of which the disease was communicated to other dogs.

If the rabid dog is not molested he will seldom attack any living object ; but the slightest obstruction in his path is sufficient to rouse his fury, and he then bites savagely, and in the most unreasoning manner, so as to be wholly uncontrollable by fear of the consequences. The gait when at liberty, is a long trot, without any deviation from the straight line, except what is compulsory from the nature of the surrounding objects.

The average time of the occurrence of rabies after the bite is, in the dog, from three weeks to six months, or possibly even longer ; so that a suspected case requires careful watching for at least that time ; but, after three months, the animal suspected to have been bitten may be considered tolerably safe.

The duration of the disease is about four or five days, but I have myself known a case fatal in forty-eight hours.

As there has never yet been discovered a cure for rabies, so the best plan in all cases is to destroy the dog as soon as he is clearly shown to exhibit the disease. In the interval he should be secluded in a safe place, where he cannot possibly get at any living animal.

INFLAMMATIONS OF THE EYE.

Ophthalmia, or simple inflammation of the eyes, is very common in the dog, especially in the latter stages of distemper, when the condition of this organ is often apparently hopeless ; though a little patience will show that no mischief eventually occurs. On more than one occasion I have saved puppies from a watery grave, whose eyes were said to be hopelessly gone.

CANKER, OR INFLAMMATION OF THE EAR.

From high feeding generally, and exposure to the weather, many dogs (especially of a sporting kind), contract an inflammation of the membrane or skin lining the ear. This produces irritation, and the dog shakes his head continually, which, together with the tendency to spread externally, causes an ulceration of the tips of the ears of those dogs, such as the hound, pointer, setter, spaniel, &c., which have these organs long and pendulous. Hence, the superficial observer is apt to confine his observation to this external observation, and I have even known the tips of the ears cut off in the hope of getting rid of the mischief, whereas it was only aggravated, because the incessant shaking caused the wound to extend, while the internal mischief was not in the slightest degree relieved.. The pointer is particularly liable to " canker," as shown on the tips of the ears, because he has little hair on this part to take off the acuteness of the " smack " which is given in the shaking of the head. Long-haired dogs on the other hand are quite as liable to the real disease, as evidenced on an examination of the internal surface ; but, from the protection afforded by the hair, the pendulous ear is not so much ulcerated or inflamed. Whenever, therefore, a dog is seen to be continually shaking his head, and abortively trying to rub or scratch his ear, not being able to succeed because he cannot reach the interior, an examination should be made of the passage leading into the head ; and if the lining is red and inflamed, there is clear evidence of the disease, even if the external ear is altogether free from it. On the other hand, the mere existence of an ulceration on the tips of the ears is no absolute proof of " canker," because it may have been caused by the briars and thorns which a spaniel or hound has to pass through in hunting for his game. Still, it should lead to a careful inspection, and if it continues for any length of time, it may be generally concluded that there is an internal cause for it.

INFLAMMATION OF THE MOUTH AND TEETH.

Dogs which are fed on strongly stimulating food are very apt to lose their teeth by decay, and also to suffer from a spongy state of the gums, attended with a collection of tartar about the roots of the teeth. Decayed teeth are better extracted, but the tartar, when it produces inflammation, may be removed by instruments if it is considered worth the trouble. By carefully scraping the teeth, there is little or no difficulty in removing it, if the dog's head is held steadily; but, few people are handy enough with the necessary tools to effect this, excepting those who make a business of the art; and, if the dog is so highly valued as to make it desirable to incur the expense, he should be taken to a veterinary surgeon.

SPASMODIC ASTHMA.

What is often called asthma in the dog, is nothing more than a permanently chronic form of bronchitis, which is very common among petted toy dogs, or house dogs, which are not alloyed much exercise. But there is a form of true asthma with spasm, which is also met with among the same kind of dogs, the *symptoms* of which are much more urgent, comprising a sudden accession of difficulty in breathing, so severe that the dog evidently gasps for breath, and yet there is no evidence of inflammation. It may be known by the suddenness of the attack, inflammation being comparatively slow in its approach.

PHTHISIS, OR CONSUMPTION.

The *symptoms* of consumption are, a slow insidious cough, without fever in the early stage, followed by emaciation, and ending after some months in diarrhœa, or exhaustion from the amount of expectoration, or in the bursting of a blood-vessel, which last is generally the termination in those dogs that are kept for use, the work to which they are subjected leading to excessive action of the heart, which is likely to burst the vessel. In the latter stages there is a good deal of constitutional fever, but it is seldom that the dog lives long enough to show this condition, being either destroyed as incurable, or dying rapidly from loss of blood or diarrhœa.

INFLAMMATION OF THE LIVER (HEPATITIS, OR YELLOWS).

This is one of the most common of the diseases to which sporting dogs are subject, in consequence of the exposure to cold and wet which they are submitted to, producing congestion of the liver, and this going on to inflammation. Dogs deprived of exercise also contract it, because their livers first becoming torpid, the bile accumulates, and then, in order to get rid of it, nature establishes an action which ends in inflammation. The *symptoms* are a yellow state of the white of the eye and skin generally, from which the disease is commonly called "the yellows."

Acute hepatitis comes on rapidly, and with a good deal of fever, generally showing itself on the day after a long exposure to wet and cold, as in shooting or hunting The dog shivers, his nose is hot, his breathing slightly quicker than usual, and his pulse quick, *small*, and *wiry*. The bowels are confined, and, when moved, the motions are clay-colored or slaty. If these symptoms are not soon relieved, the case ends fatally, sickness coming on, and the strength being rapidly exhausted.

INFLAMMATION OF THE BOWELS.

Four varieties of this condition are met with, viz. : 1, acute inflammation of the peritonæal coat ; 2, spasms of the muscular coat, attended with congestion or inflammation, and known as *colic ;* 3, inflammation of the mucous coat, attended by *diarrhœa ;* and 4, chronic inflammation, almost always followed by constipation.

Acute inflammation of the peritonæal coat is known as *peritonitis* and *enteritis*, according as its attacks are confined to the membrane lining the general cavity (*peritonæum*), or to that covering the intestines (*enteron*) ; but, as there is seldom one without more or less of the other, there is little practical use in the distinction. The *symptoms* are very severe, and are shown by shivering, feverishness, cold dry nose, ears, and legs, breath hot, and the expression anxious, showing evidence of pain, which is increased on pressing the bowels with the hand. The tail is kept closely pressed against the body, and the attitude is peculiar to the disease, the back being arched, and the legs all drawn together. The bowels are costive, the urine scanty and high-colored ; there is thirst, and the appetite is absent altogether. Sometimes there is a slight vomiting after food, but at others it is retained ; though, in the later stages, the former condition generally prevails. The disease soon runs on, and, if not relieved, is fatal in a few days.

Colic is also a frequent complaint among the dog tribe, the *signs* being intense pain aggravated at intervals to such a degree as to cause the patient to howl most loudly, the back being at the same time arched as far as possible, and the legs drawn together. If this shows itself suddenly after a

full meal, the colic may at once be surmised to exist, but the howl at first
is not very loud, the dog starting up with a sharp moan, and then lying
down again, to repeat the start and moan in a few minutes with increased
intensity, until it becomes a howl continued for many seconds together.
The nose is of a natural appearance, and there is little or no fever, the evidence of pain being all that directs the attention to the bowels, where there
is no tenderness, and, on the contrary, pressure gradually made with the
hand seems to afford relief.

Chronic inflammation with constipation is very apt to occur in dogs
which are not exercised, and are fed with biscuit or meal without vegeta-
bles. The consequence is, that the bowels after a time become inflamed,
and diarrhœa is set up; but, this soon ceasing, the mucous membrane is
impaired in tone, and there is a want of the proper secretion, so that the
fœces become hard, and the muscular coat refuses to act as it should do.
In such a case, the belly becomes distended, and there is excessive pain,
with more or less spasm. In some instances the *fœces* have become so im-
pacted that no means could be used which would overcome the mechanical
difficulty, and the dogs have died "undelivered." It is easy to distinguish
these collections, because they may be readily felt through the flank, and
nothing but a case of pregnancy can be mistaken for them.

SKIN DISEASES.

Almost all skin diseases depend on neglect in some form; and in the
dog they arise either from improper management, as in the case of
"blotch," or "surfeit," or from the presence of parasites, as in mange.
These three names are all that are applied to skin diseases in the dog,
though there can be no doubt that they vary greatly, and mange itself
is subdivided by different writers so as to comprehend several varieties.
Fleas, ticks, &c., also irritate the skin greatly, and all will therefore
be included here, the inflammation produced by them being entitled to
be considered a skin disease as much as mange itself.

Blotch, or *surfeit*, shows itself in the shape of scabby lumps of matted hair, on the back, sides, head, and quarters, as well as occasionally
on the inside of the thighs. They vary from the size of a sixpence to
that of half a crown, are irregularly round in shape, and after about
three or four days the scab and hair fall off, leaving the skin bare, red,
and slightly inclined to discharge a thin serum. The disease is not contagious, and evidently arises from gross feeding, joined very frequently
with want of exercise, and often brought out by a gallop after long confinement to the kennel.

An eruption between the toes, similar in its nature and cause to
"blotch," is also very common. showing itself chiefly at the roots of the
nails, where there are considerable redness and swelling, and so much
tenderness as to make the dog quite lame. In bad cases, when the

constitution is impaired by defective kennel arrangements, the sores become very foul, and are then very difficult to heal.

Foul mange (resembling the *psoriasis* of man in its nature) is a most unmanageable disease, inasmuch as it has become quite constitutional before it can be so designated, and because, being a disease of the blood, it requires a complete change in the composition of this fluid before it can be eradicated. It is doubtful whether mange is contagious, but that it is hereditary I have no doubt whatever, the proofs within my own knowledge being amply sufficient to convince me of the fact. Thus I have seen a bitch apparently cured of it, and with a perfectly healthy skin, produce a litter of whelps all of which broke out with mange at four or five months old, though scattered in various parts of the country at their walks; the bitch afterwards showing the impurity of her blood by again and again becoming the subject of mange. I should therefore never breed from either a dog or bitch who was attacked by this form of eruption. There is considerable thickening of the skin, with an offensive discharge from the surface, chiefly flowing from the cracks and ulcerations under the scabs on it. This dries and falls off in scales, taking with them a good deal of the hair, which is further removed by the constant scratching of the poor dog, who is tormented with incessant itching. Almost always there is a fat, unwieldy state of the system, from want of exercise, but the appetite is often deficient.

Virulent mange (which may be compared to *psora* and *porrigo* in the human subject) is of two kinds, one attributable to a parasitic insect, and the other of vegetable origin. In the former case, which is its most common form, it appears in large kennels where cleanliness is not sufficiently attended to, and when the floors become loaded with the excretions. There is no doubt that this is highly contagious, but there is also little difference of opinion as to its being capable of being bred or developed among a lot of previously healthy dogs if mismanaged in the above way. The skin shows itself bare of hair in large patches of irregular form, and the hair being as it were gradually worn away at the edges, as if by scratching. The skin is dry and rough, with cracks and creases in various directions, from some of which a thin ichorous discharge may be seen to flow, on removing the scabs which fill them. The dog feeds well, but from want of sleep is languid and listless; there is considerable thirst and some slight feverishness, but very often the flesh is maintained for months at a high rate. The *treatment* of this form of mange is founded upon the belief that it is caused by an insect of the *acarus* tribe, which has been detected by the microscope in many cases, but which by some people is maintained to be an accidental effect, and not a cause of mange.

CHOREA.

Chorea, or *St. Vitus's dance*, may be known by the spasmodic twitches which accompany it, and by their ceasing during sleep. In slight cases the spasm is a mere drop of the head and shoulder, or some-times of the hind quarter only, giving a very silly and weak expression to the animal. Chorea is almost always a consequence of distemper, so that it is unnecessary to describe its early stages, and the disease itself cannot be further defined than by the above description. It seldom goes on to destroy life, though occasionally it is accompanied by fits, the disease in the brain and spine then being of such a severe nature as to end fatally in the course of time, the dog apparently dying from exhaustion. Of the exact nature of the disease we know nothing—the most careful examination of the brain and spinal cord leading to no useful result. But it often happens that there is present at the same time a degree of mischief in the stomach, caused apparently by the presence of worms, and then the chorea is said to be sympathetic with this.

SHAKING PALSY.

This resembles chorea in its nature, but it is incessant, except during sleep, and attacks the whole body. The *same remedies* may be applied, but it is an incurable disease, though not always destroying life.

WORMS.

Worms are a fertile source of disease in the dog, destroying every year more puppies than the distemper itself; and, in spite of every pre-caution, appearing in the kennelled hound or shooting-dog, as well as the pampered house-pet and the half-starved cur.

The *symptoms* of the presence of worms in the dog should be carefully noted and anxiously looked for, if the health of the animal is of any importance. They are, an unhealthy appearance of the coat, the hair looking dead and not lying smoothly and evenly; appetite ravenous in proportion to the condition, which is generally low, though worms may exist for months without interfering much with the presence of fat. After a time, however, the fat of the body is absorbed, and the muscles, without being firm and prominent, are marked with intervening lines from its absence. The *fœces* are passed frequently and in small quanti-ties, the separate passage of a small quantity of mucus each time being particularly indicative of worms, especially if there is first a solid lump, and then a small portion of frothy mucus. The spirits are also dull, the nose hot and dry, and the breath offensive. These signs are only present to the full extent when the dog is troubled with tape-worm, or with the round-worm in large quantities; the maw-worm being only slightly injurious in comparison with the others, and seldom producing the whole of the above train of symptoms. The kidney-worm, of course, has no effect upon the intestinal secretions, but it produces bloody urine, more or less mixed with *pus*. Still, as these are often present without this worm, it is impossible to predict its existence during life, with any degree of certainty.

INDIGESTION (Dyspepsia).

Among the most common consequences of improper feeding and neglect of exercise is indigestion, attended by its usual concomitant, constipation. It shows itself in flatulence, loss of appetite, alternations of constipation and diarrhœa, low spirits, and want of muscular vigor; although often the animal is fat enough, or, indeed, sometimes loaded with fat (adipose matter). Such a state of things never occurs to a dog properly reared and afterwards well managed, being confined to those which are either fed on improper food, or allowed too much of it, or which are not allowed exercise enough ; or, as is too frequently the case, which are submitted to all three of these causes.

UNNATURAL PARTURITION.

I have heretofore alluded to the management of healthy parturition, but in this chapter I must say something of the proper conduct to be observed where the process is disturbed by any accidental complication. As, however, these unnatural labors only occur in any number to the veterinary practitioner, I shall take the liberty of inserting here Mr. Youatt's remarks on the subject, which I believe to be truthful throughout :—

"The pupping usually takes place from the sixty-second to the sixty-fourth day.; and, the process having commenced, from a quarter to three quarters of an hour generally takes place between the production of each puppy.

"Great numbers of bitches are lost every year in the act of parturition: there seems to be a propensity in the females to associate with dogs larger than themselves, and they pay for it with their lives. The most neglected circumstance during the period of pregnancy is the little exercise which the mother is permitted to take, while, in point of fact, nothing tends more to safe and easy parturition than her being permitted or compelled to take a fair quantity of exercise.

"When the time of parturition has arrived, and there is evident difficulty in producing the fœtus, recourse should be had to the ergot of rye, which should be given every hour or half hour, according to circumstances. If after a certain time some, although little, progress has been made, the ergot must be continued in smaller doses, or perhaps suspended for a while ; but, if all progress is evidently suspended, recourse must be had to the hook or the forceps. By gentle but continued manipulation much may be done, especially when the muzzle of the puppy can be brought into the passage. As little force as possible must be used, and especially the fœtus little broken. Many a valuable animal is destroyed by the undue application of force.

"If the animal seems to be losing strength, a small quantity of laudanum and ether may be administered. ' The patience of bitches in labor is extreme,' says Mr. Blaine ; ' and their distress, if not removed, is most striking and affecting. Their luck is at such time particularly expressive and apparently imploring.' When the pupping is protracted, and the young ones are evidently dead, the mother may be saved, if none of the puppies have been broken. In process of time the different puppies may, one after another, be extracted ; but when violence has been used at the commencement, or almost at any part of the process, death will assuredly follow.

"*Jan.* 15, 1876. —- A terrier bitch was brought to my repository to-day, who has been in great and constant pain since yesterday, making repeated but fruitless efforts to expel her puppies. She is in a very plethoric habit of body ; her bowels are much confined, and she exhibits some general symptoms of febrile derangement, arising, doubtless, from her protracted labor, This is her first litter. Upon examination no young could be distinctly felt.

" Place her in a warm bath, and give her a dose of castor oil, morning and evening.

"*Jan.* 16.—The bitch appears in the same state as yesterday, except that the medicine has operated freely upon the bowels, and the febrile symptoms have somewhat decreased. Her strainings are as frequent and distressing as ever. Take two scruples of the ergot of rye, and divide into six doses, of which let one be given every half hour.

" In about ten minutes after the exhibition of the last dose of this medicine, she brought forth, with great difficulty, one dead puppy ; upon taking which away from her, she became so uneasy that I was induced to return it to her. In about a quarter of an hour after this I paid her another visit ; the puppy could not now be found ; but a suspicious appearance in the mother's eye betrayed at once that she had devoured it. I immediately administered an emetic ; and in a very short time the whole fœtus was returned in five distinct parts, viz., the four quarters and the head. After this, the bitch began to amend very fast ; she produced no other puppy ; and, as her supply of milk was small, she was soon convalescent."

www.ingramcontent.com/pod-product-compliance
Lightning Source LLC
Chambersburg PA
CBHW021429090426
42739CB00009B/1415